SWEDEN

LAND OF THE MIDNIGHT SUN

*Du gamla, du fria, du fjällhöga Nord
du tysta du glädjerika sköna!*

Distributed by:

 Ultraförlaget AB

Svetsarvägen 18
hone 46-8-983330 Fax 46-8-297550
S-17141 SOLNA
SWEDEN

Published and printed by

NARNI - TERNI

D1307480

TEXT: **Martina Forti - Stefania Belloni**
ENGLISH TEXT: **Prof. Brian Williams**

OUR WARMEST THANKS ARE DUE TO:
for their kind collaboration in the production of this book and for the concession of the photographs mentioned below.
  - Ms. **Astrid Lindgren**, through the Agency **Kerstin Kvint** for permission to reproduce the drawing on page 11
  - **The Swedish Match Co.** for the photo on page 82
  - **Tetrapak Italia s.p.a.** for the photo on page 8/2
  - **The Swedish Tourist Board of Milan**
  - **The Swedish Tourist Board of Stockholm**

PHOTOGRAPHS:
  Swedish Tourist Board of Milan:
      pages 5, 7, 14, 36/3, 37/2, 38/1, 41/2, 44/2, 52/1, 56/1, 63/3, 68/2.

  Hans Hammarskiöld (for the Vasa Museum):
      pages 27, 29.

Ultraförlaget:
      back of cover 2, pages 2, 6, 13, 33, 38/2, 39, 44/1, 58/2, 73/1, 90/2.

Focus Team:
      cover, pages 1, 4, 8/1, 9, 10, 15, 19, 19/1, 47/2, 49/1, 51, 52/2, 65, 66, 67, 71, 79/2, 88, 89, 91/2, 92.

Pagani:
      pages 59, 61/2, 83, 84, 85, 86, 87.

Plurigraf:
      back of cover, pages 12, 16, 17, 18, 20, 21, 22, 23, 24, 25, 26, 28, 30, 31, 32, 34, 35, 40, 41, 42, 43, 45, 46, 47/1, 48, 49, 50, 53, 54, 55, 56, 57, 60, 61, 68/1, 69, 70, 72, 73/2, 73/3, 74, 75, 76, 77, 78, 80, 81, 90/1, 93, 94, 95, 96.

Index

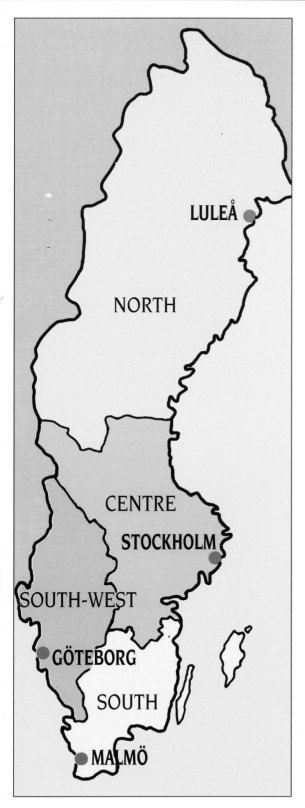

The biggest country in the Scandinavian peninsula and one of the largest in Europe, Sweden is a fascinating mix of rugged, unspoilt natural beauty, ancient, deep-rooted traditions, thriving arts and culture and one of the most civic-minded and democratic peoples in the world.

The total area of Sweden is 450,000 sq.km, extending from the Skåne region in the south up to Lapland in the north. Three states, Sweden, Norway and Finland, meet at the most northerly point of Lapland. The country borders on Norway to the west and north and Finland to the northeast and is washed on the southwest by the North Sea, on the southeast by the Baltic Sea and on the east by the Gulf of Bothnia. Despite its great size, Sweden has a population of only 8 million (including 17,000 Same or Laplanders), mostly concentrated in the southern and central regions.

In the capital, Stockholm, alone, there are 1,500,000 people, while Lapland, the huge northern part, is almost completely uninhabited. Sweden is divided into 25 provinces, and for administrative purposes, into 24 counties. For the purposes of tourism however, the country may be divided into four main areas of interest.

These are Southern Sweden with its castles and old crystal factories, the West Coast with its archaeological sites and cave paintings, Central Sweden with its folklore and Northern Sweden, home to groups of Same who still live according to age-old traditions and customs.

GEOGRAPHY AND CLIMATE

The geological formation of the country was laid down about 2 1/2 billion years ago but the topography was determined during the glaciation period.

The North is almost entirely covered by the Scandinavian Mountain chain, whose highest peak is Mount Kebneikaise (2,111 m). Towards the south, the mountains give way to extensive uplands, formed by repeated glacial movement, and hilly areas which slope gradually down towards the coast. The great lakes in the central part of the country – Lake Vänern, the third largest in Europe, Lake Vättern and Lake Mälaren – bear witness to the fact that this area was once below sea level. The earliest prehistoric settlements grew up on the shores of these lakes where the present capital, Stockholm, is situated today. Rivers are numerous and provide an important source of hydroelectric power and an efficient transport system for the timber industry, although the fishing has been greatly reduced due to pollution.

Thanks to the influence of the Gulf Stream, the country's climate is temperate, but varies from region to region.

The winters are long and severe, the summers brief and intense, but while there are four fairly definite seasons in the South, in the North it can snow even in mid-August!

In the area north of the Arctic Circle, the sun never shines all winter long but in the summer, between mid-May and mid-July the so-called "midnight sun" shines without interruption for 24 hours on end.

The features of the Swedish climate include wind and rain and it is perhaps for this reason that the weather is one of the Swedish people's favourite topics of conversation.

When they go on holidays, Swedes choose destinations such as Spain, Italy and other countries which boast, besides ancient cultural traditions, a mild climate and plenty of sunshine.

The Swedes also like warm colours and a welcoming atmosphere when decorating their houses and wood, ceramics and pastel colours are predominant. The comfortable and reassuring images found in Swedish homes have been portrayed with great realism by two of the most important national painters, Carl Larsson, to whom we owe a series of water-colours dedicated, in fact, to the "house", and Anders Zorn.

THE SOCIAL SYSTEM

One of the principal interests of the Swedish government is the health and well-being of the country's citizens. Sweden boasts one of the best welfare systems in the world.

The health care system, schools and public services are extremely efficient, even the prisons are like luxurious hotels.

Disabled citizens are particularly well cared for. Every building is equipped to allow wheelchair access, lifts have been altered to make movement easier and footpaths have been built so as not to be an obstacle for the visually impaired.

Many hotels have rooms adapted for disabled people and even for those suffering from allergies.

Such an efficient system does entail extremely high taxes, and Swedes pay up to 80% of their salaries to the government.

Such severe economic conditions could only be accepted in a country where the people naturally respect law and order, punctuality and the opinions of others. This does not mean that Swedes are serious or inflexible people. On the contrary they love company, parties, drinking sessions and irony, but above all they love nature and the healthy life.

The country's attractions include numerous open air sports and relaxing country and seaside resorts. Even communication is not difficult for visitors to Sweden since everyone knows at least one other language besides their own.

Today, tourists seek one of the symbols of Sweden, the little Dalarna horse, a carved and painted wooden horse, whose origins go back to the XVIII century, when woodcutters made toys for their children. This tradition is still kept alive today in Nusnas, a village near Mora.

Golf is a very popular sport in Sweden, thanks in part to Annika Sörenstam and Liselotte Neuman, two Swedish players of world fame.

The official language is Swedish, which belongs to the North Germanic linguistic family.

It is a sing-song language, very pleasant to the ear, and contains many words borrowed from other languages such as English, which is perfectly spoken all over Sweden and taught from the very first year of school onwards.

Lapp dialect or Finnish is only spoken in a few areas in the North and the written language is always Swedish. Lutheranism is the official religion although Roman Catholic and Jewish minorities do exist.

The currency used is the Swedish krona, divided into 100 öre. Like the other Scandinavian countries, the Swedish flag represents the Christian symbol of the cross, in this case yellow on a blue background.

The Swedish are deeply attached to their traditions and the flag is flown with great pomp and circumstance on the 6 June, the national holiday.

The Royal Family

There is great love for the royal family despite the fact that the monarchy today has only symbolic value.

Since the country is a constitutional monarchy, the king performs honorary duties only. Legislative power is in the hands of Parliament and executive power in those of the Cabinet of Ministers, presided over by the Prime Minister who is the leader of the majority party.

The present king, **Carl Gustav XVI**, is married to **Queen Sylvia** and is father to three children. He was crowned in 1973 when the former king, Gustav Adolphus VI, known all over Europe, and especially in Italy, for his interest in archaeology, died and left him the throne.

The ancient splendour of the Swedish monarchy survives today in the official symbol of Sweden: the three-pointed crown, a reminder of when the country was made up of three kingdoms, the Goter, the Svear and the Vendel.

Nature and the Swedes

The Swedish people maintain that the water in their rivers and lakes is still pure enough to drink without any problem. Although this seems an exaggerated statement, it is in fact true that, at least in Lapland, the countryside is so unspoilt and human activity so minimal that the region has remained a real natural paradise.

Moreover, Stockholm is one of the few capitals in the world where the inhabitants can swim in local waters and off the surrounding islands.

All this is possible thanks to the great consideration that the Swedish people devote to the problem of protecting the environment. The rules governing environmental protection are very strict and are applied rigorously.

Swedish people's civic-minded-

The royal family of Sweden celebrates the eighteenth birthday of Princess Victoria.

THE SWEDISH NATIONAL ANTHEM

The Swedish national anthem came into being by wedding a popular tune to a text written by the expert on folklore and ballads, Richard Dybeck (1811-1877).

The popularity of this fine popular song spread so far and wide that it eventually became the national anthem.

**Du gamla, du fria, du fjällhöga Nord
du tysta du glädjerika sköna!
Jag hälsar dig, vänaste land uppå jord,
din sol, din himmel, dina ängder gröna**

**You ancient, free land of the Mountains of the North,
Silent and fair and radiant!
I greet thee, land most beloved on earth,
your sun, your skies, your smiling green fields.**

(Free translation)

Wandering among the woods and mountains is one of the favourite leisure-time occupations of the Swedes.

ness is witnessed by the "Alleman-sratt", literally "rights that belong to everyone", an ancient custom that gives everyone the right to walk in the countryside, even across other people's land, on condition of course that no damage is done.

By the year 2010 Sweden will have no nuclear power stations, concentrating finances and resources on alternative sources of energy.

In the meantime a campaign has been set up to curb the acidification of the lakes and sulphur, nitrate and oxide emissions which cause the death of great numbers of fish and permanently pollute the waters.

The Swedish landscape varies greatly due to the fact the the country lies partly in central Europe and partly in the most northern area of Western civilisation, beyond the Arctic Circle.

The vegetation in the extreme North is subarctic and is characterised by tundra, mosses and lichens.

A little further south in Norrland there are immense forests (covering 50% of the country's total area!) made up of pines, firs and birches, beautiful trees with silver bark which are a feature of all Scandinavian lands.

In the centre of the country and as far as the extreme South, as the mountains and upland areas gradually recede, they are replaced by vast areas under crops (in fact the Skane region is known as the bread basket of Sweden) as well as deciduous forests of oak, ash, elm and beech.

Like all Scandinavians, Swedes love colour and it is quite common to find large areas unfarmed and full of flowers,which become breathtakingly beautiful close to the sea (like the countless orchids and roses on the island of Gotland).

The carved wooden houses have balconies full of flowers, just like the ones immortalised by the great Swedish artist, Carl Larsson, in his paintings, now on display in

the Sundborn museum in Dalarnia. In any case, all Swedes feel a great need to spend as much time as possible outdoors.

At weekends, when work is over, there is a veritable exodus from the cities towards country homes and rustic chalets (which can also be rented by tourists).

These holiday homes are simple but have all modern conveniences and are found in wonderful locations.

Here, in woods rich with strawberries, blueberries, raspberries and mushrooms (the famous "strawberry places" immortalised in the well-known Ingmar Bergman film), Swedes devote themselves to their favourite activities, cycling and countless other open-air sports both on land and sea.

Sweden's natural heritage is completed and enriched by a great variety of fauna. Reindeers, all domestic by now, are numerous (270,000 in Swedish territory) and are one of the main sources of income for the Same.

Many people enjoy fishing, canoeing and sailing on the numerous lakes in Sweden; these activities are all greatly loved by the Swedes.

In the long Arctic winter, herds of reindeer can be seen migrating towards the coniferous forests on the Norrland border.

All arctic animals live in reserves, national parks or protected areas (roughly 5% of the total land area). Even the musk ox can still be found, although in greatly diminished numbers. Moles, bats, storks and swans are found in the more southern regions.

Numerous sea urchins live off the island of Gotland but seals are rarely found now in the Baltic Sea. Pike and salmon live in the rivers and lakes and the sea is full of perch and other types of fish, but Sweden is above all a paradise for ornithologists, thanks to the presence of an extraordinary number of birds. The chaffinch, the snipe, the lapwing and the herring gull are among the more common species.

The love of nature and the open-air life is a distinctive characteristic of the Swedish people and this was so even in the past.

It is no surprise that one of the most famous naturalists of all time was the Swedish doctor, Carl von Linne (1707-1778), better known all over the world as Linnaeus.

THE ECONOMY

Sweden is the richest of the Scandinavian countries and one of the most industrialised nations in the world, despite the fact that only one century ago it was one of the poorest countries in Europe and about one fifth of the population was forced to emigrate across the Atlantic.

In fact, in particular from the province of Småland, more than 35,000 Swedes set sail for Illinois, Minnesota, Kansas and Canada and, in small groups, almost all parts of the United States.

There, they founded colonies and intermarried with the local populations.

One of the descendants of these early Swedish settlers was John Morton, one of the signatories of the Declaration of Independence. As modern industry gradually developed and railways were built, rural communities became less isolated and the flux of emigrants began to diminish.

Around 1890, industry became the main national source of income and entire regions, once agricultural, became highly industrialised.

Sweden is now one of the major producers of iron in Europe, thanks to the ample Kiruna and Gallivare deposits in Lapland. Other mineral resources are copper, lead, zinc, tungsten, gold and silver.

Agriculture is still an important sector in the Swedish economy. Farming was practised in Sweden as far back as 3,000 BC!

Today intelligent land use and highly sophisticated technology means that although only scanty space is available (6.6% of the total area), wheat, barley, rye, oats, potatoes and sugarbeet are grown.

Cattle-rearing is closely tied to the growing of forage crops and

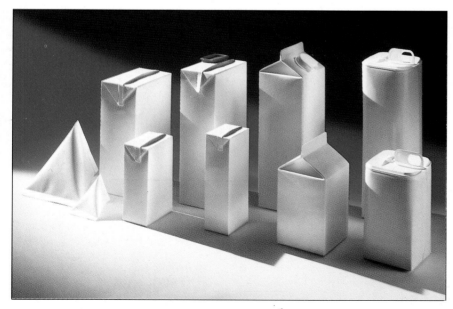

A Tetra Pack container. These practical containers, of purely Swedish conception, are now used in everyday life all over the world.

is almost exclusively orientated towards the production of milk and dairy products.

The immense forests, extensively, but intelligently, exploited, provide large quantities of timber, generally for use in national industry.

Swedish furniture and household objects can now be found all over the world and represent a school of design that is the pride of nearly all Scandinavia.

The main Swedish industries are however metallurgy and machinery (especially the production of machines for treating paper and wood and for producing ball-bearings), weapons, aircraft, transport and shipbuilding.

The motor industry, whose Volvos and Saabs are known all over the world, deserves a special mention. It is specialising more and more in the production of industrial vehicles. Thanks to the country's immense water resources, Sweden is autonomous in the production of hydroelectric power, although this cannot be said for the burning of fossil fuels which have to be imported.

In the last few years the tourist industry has prospered.

All over Sweden there are first class hotels, campsites, hostels and holiday homes (chalets and cottages to rent) and excellent sporting facilities – the pride of the country.

Among other activities it is worth mentioning game fishing, skiing, rafting and canoeing on the country's numerous lakes and rivers.

The country is efficiently served by an extensive air, rail and shipping network.

Very attentive to the problems of the disabled, the Swedes have recently published a "Holiday Guide for Disabled" with a list of activities and places where the disabled are welcome.

SWEDEN AND ITS IMPORTANT CULTURAL HERITAGE

"Give me a whiskey with ginger ale on the side and don't be stingy, baby!" Although this was the first line spoken by the woman who Winston Churchill defined as "the most fascinating of all time", this takes nothing from the charm and elegance of the great Swedish actress, **Greta Garbo**.

Along with many other Swedish actresses such as Ingrid Bergman, **Anita Ekberg**, **Bibi Anderson**, **Britt Ekland**, she contributed to the fame of Swedish actresses, whose talent, grace and beauty is recognised all over the world.

Sweden has always contributed greatly to the cinema and the the-

In the last thirty years the number of protected zones and natural reserves in Swedish territory has increased very substantially. At the moment there are more than 1300 natural reserves in the country. There are also 22 national parks, and many others are planned for the future.

Pippi Longstocking, one of the amusing characters created by the imagination of the authoress Astrid Lindgren.

atre and is home to highly-talented actors and actresses, directors and directors of photography who work all over the world and are extremely well-known and greatly admired.

The most famous include the director **Ingemar Bergman**, the actor **Max von Sidow** and the director of photography **Sven Nykvist.**

All Swedish cities possess modern, efficient facilities for film, theatre, music and ballet (the "Cullberg" company in Stockholm is very famous) and the cultural season all over Sweden is rich and varied.

Music festivals are numerous, both in summer and winter, and jazz is particularly popular, although Swedish people appreciate all types of music including classical, rock and folk.

All the arts are highly appreciated and the State provides study grants and annuities so that artists and writers can follow their vocation without hindrance.

Every time a book is borrowed from a library a small sum is paid to the author, a custom Sweden shares with the other Scandinavian countries.

Particular attention is paid to children's education; one of the most important children's story writers in the world is: Astrid Lindgren. Her books such as Pippi Longstocking, Rasmus and the Tramp and Holiday on Gull Island and many others, have been translated in more than 70 countries, even into Zulu! In Vimmerby, where Astrid Lindgren was born, a miniature village has been built and peopled with the characters from her novels.

By now, almost ninety and practically blind, Ms Lindgren is so highly considered by the Swedish people that she is consulted even on government matters concerning environment, education and other topics.

One of the most important Swedish literary figures is without doubt the story teller and playwright AUGUST STRINDBERG (1849-1912).

His work is the expression of the darkest, most sombre, pessimistic and tormented aspect of the Swedish soul.

A great misogynist, one of his most famous characters is actually a woman, created in "Miss Julie".

Human nature, at its most tragic in the great lonely and melancholic North, has found its truest expression in the works of Strindberg.

THE NOBEL PRIZE

Another important character in Swedish cultural life and in a certain sense in research all over the world is Alfred Nobel. In 1895, one year before his death, Nobel made a will in which he declared that the greater part of his estate should become an investment fund.

The proceeds from such investment were, in his own words, "to be distributed annually in the form of a prize to those who had contributed, in the course of that year, to the well-being of humanity... whether they were Scandinavian or not".

The five human activities that Nobel wished to encourage were physics, chemistry, physiology or medicine, literature and fraternity between peoples (peace).

The will entrusted the duty of assigning the prizes to three Swedish institutions and to a special commission elected by the Norwegian Parliament, given that at the time Sweden and Norway were united in the one kingdom.

Nobel entrusted the choice of candidates for the Peace Prize to the Norwegians and they have fulfilled his mandate ever since.

The prize-giving ceremony takes place simultaneously in Stockholm and Oslo, in the presence of both royal families, every year on the 10 December, the anniversary of Nobel's death.

Among the Nobel prizes awarded to Sweden, one in particular is worth mentioning. In 1909, the Nobel prize for literature was awarded to **Selma Lagerlöf**, authoress of the famous "Gösta Berling Saga", a popular epic which transports us to the romantic but sombre atmosphere of nineteenth century Sweden. The writer's home, now transformed into a museum, can be visited in Marbacka, a small town near Lake Vänern.

FESTIVALS AND POPULAR TRADITIONS

Another of the many Swedish summer events, the Stockholm Water Festival.

The extreme variety in the geography of the country has meant that popular customs and traditions differ from place to place, even though there is a great desire to make them uniform. The Valpurga Festival for example, celebrated on the 30 April, is one of the most important festivities in the land because it announces the arrival of spring, although in some parts of the country it is still so cold that the ground is covered in snow and people have to wear thick jumpers and furs to keep warm. It is a pecularity of Sweden that many feast-days are linked to the Catholic religious tradition and even to pagan festivals, despite the fact that Lutheranism was introduced into the country five centuries ago. Many of these feasts have been thus "adapted" to the new calendar with minor adjustments although the character and meaning of the ritual remain unaltered. As in many other countries, Sweden too celebrates with great participation and lavishness the traditional Christian feasts such as Christmas and Easter, but another two very original celebrations, the Feast of St Lucia and the Feast of St John or Midsummer, are of great interest to the visitor.

FEAST OF ST. LUCIA

The Feast of St Lucia is celebrated on the 13 December, the longest night of the year, in memory of the winter solstice. On the morning of the 13 December, all over Sweden, in houses, offices, schools, factories and farms, a young girl dressed in a long white dress with a red belt and a crown of candles on her head, goes from one room to another offering everyone special cakes, ginger biscuits and saffron brioches, coffee and glögg, a hot spiced wine. In 1928, one of the major Swedish dailies, "Stockholm's Dagblad" announced a beauty contest to elect the Stockholm Lucia. Since then various young girls have been selected to bear the title Lucia after a long series of tests. The lit candles that they bear on their heads symbolise the light that vanquishes the evil forces of night and winter until the return of the luminous spring days.

MIDSUMMER FESTIVAL

The summer is characterised by the Feast of St John or Midsummer celebrated on the Saturday closest to the 24 June. Like the Feast of St Lucia, that of St John too is an exaltation of light as the opposite to the darkness of winter. On this occasion, houses, churches, streets, public squares and even cars are decorated with plants and flowers and all the celebrations take place outdoors and in particular around the "Maypole". This is a pole decorated with branches and flowers set up in every city, town and village. Around the Maypole, symbol of summer and nature's reawakening, dances are performed, games are played and songs are sung all through the night, to celebrate "Midsummer's Eve". Tradition holds that the night of St John has magic powers. It is believed for example that the dew that falls during the night is a miraculous drug and that if seven different types of flowers are collected in as many different fields, tied in one bunch and placed under the pillow, a man or woman will dream of the person they will marry. Food too is important on this occasion and traditional dishes include herrings prepared in different ways, new potatoes and giant strawberries. Moreover, like all nations that enjoy company, drinking with friends and having a good time, the Swedish people care about good food and their national dishes are the richest and most varied of all the Scandinavian countries.

THE SWEDISH CUISINE

The mixture of sweet and sour is a feature of Swedish cooking; thus it is not rare to find dishes based on meat and fish cooked with salt and sugar, spices and even blueberries, cream or apple sauce.

The classic Swedish meal is the **SMÖRGÅSBORD**, a rich buffet with all types of food where everyone serves themselves as much as they like. Herrings, prepared in different ways, smoked and marinated salmon and other fish depending on the season, sardines and eels are always present.

Fresh prawns deserve a special mention, they are so popular in Sweden that there is a festival in their honour. From the second Wednesday in August onwards, prawn fishing is permitted; every evening people meet, wearing strange hats and paper napkins, to fish for these delicacies, now becoming rarer all the time.

They are eaten with bread and cheese or cooked with dill, and accompanied by beer and akvavit. Meat, too, is always part of the Smörgåsbord buffet and popular dishes include liver pate, ham, steak, smoked reindeer and different types of meatballs and sausage. Vegetable dishes are mainly salads, cabbage, potatoes, spinach and mashed potatoes.

Cheese is usually served at the end of a good meal. There are many types of fresh bread, white, rye and dill, but the most famous feature of Swedish cooking is the round crispbread with the hole in the middle.

Long ago, every kitchen table had a pole that the bread was kept on. In the evening the Swedes eat a full meal but at lunchtime they prefer something quick and easy. Restaurants include many typical Swedish dishes on their menus. These include *crayfish*, a soup made with pork and peas, *"pannkakor"* which are pancakes of all types, *"rarakor"*, pork fritters, *"pytt-i-panna"*, stew with egg and peas and *"kaldalmar"*, cabbage rolls. Goose is often eaten in the South, reindeer and capercaillie in the North and trout, herring and cod in the central parts of the country.

Beer, particularly lager and pils, in strong, medium and light versions, and Snaps, the famous potent akvavit, are drunk all over Sweden. As in many other countries, in Sweden it is not permitted to drink alcoholic drinks at all times of the day. Alcohol is not served before mid-day, unless you buy a bottle in a shop with a "Systembolaget" sign. You must be over twenty to do so.

The great variety of food, cultural traditions, customs, landscapes and people in Sweden offers the visitor a kaleidoscopic vision of many images, from the warm welcoming atmosphere of the South to the lively stimulating central regions to the fascinating mysterious silence of the Great North, far from our chaotic civilisations, where it is still possible to feel at one with nature.

Knäckebröd, the Swedish cracker, is a typical product of the Swedish export market.

STOCKHOLM

Stockholm, capital of Sweden, seat of Parliament and government and home to the royal family, is one of the most fascinating and attractive cities in Europe. The city is built on 14 islands between Lake Mälaren and the Baltic Sea, in an archipelago of 24,000 islands.

Water makes up a third of the surface area of the city and its seven districts – Gamla Stan, Norrmalm, Södermalm, Östermalm, Vasastan, Kungsholmen and Djurgården – are linked together by a dense network of bridges, piers and canals that has earned Stockholm the name "Venice of the North".

Founded by Birger Jarl in 1252, on the site of an old Viking settlement, the city grew up around a fortress built to defend the merchants in the area from enemy attacks from the sea. Stockholm was made capital city only in 1523 by King Gustav Vasa who freed the country from the Danes.

From that moment on, Stockholm really began to grow and has developed harmoniously up to the present day, despite numerous fires which razed it to the ground several times. Today it is a city with plenty of open space (about a third of the land area is made up of parks and gardens), big and small shopping centres, bars, restaurants, theatres, art galleries and museums.

The latter include the "Modern Art Museum" which boasts an enviable collection of twentieth century art, with works by Picasso, Dali and Warhol; the "Skansen" which contains 140 reconstructed buildings of great historic and ethnographic value from all over Sweden and the "Strindberg Museum", set in the "Blue Tower", last home of the famous Swedish writer, with all his furniture and personal effects.

Stockholm also contains what is known as "the biggest art gallery in the world" – the underground, whose stations have been decorated with total freedom by more than 70 artists in all mediums. Modern architectural expression is

at its most daring in the "Globen", which has quickly become the symbol of the city.

This is an enormous steel, reinforced concrete and glass sphere, (the largest spherical construction in the world!). The Globen is used for cultural and sporting events and can hold up to 16,000 spectators.

Ancient and modern, severe and unpredictable, Stockholm is at its most fascinating in summer, when the streets, squares and canals are filled with people and boats of all types and all kinds of activities are taking place. A famous meeting place is the Kungsträdgården, the most lively public gardens in the city, situated on the island of Norrmalm. In the winter, there is ice-skating while in the summer, there is always a concert, a ballet or some other cultural event taking place.

The great love of water which dominates the lives of the city's inhabitants is celebrated in summer during the nine days of the "Stockholm Water Festival".

This is an exaltation of parties, fireworks, regattas and shows during which a prize is awarded to the most distinguished person in hydro-ecological research.

Stockholm has been nominated Cultural Capital of Europe 1998.
With more than 70 different stages, Stockholm has one of the highest theatre densities of all European cities. Here, more than 1,500 visual artists and craftsmen live and work. Here, too, there are nearly 60 museums and numerous art galleries.

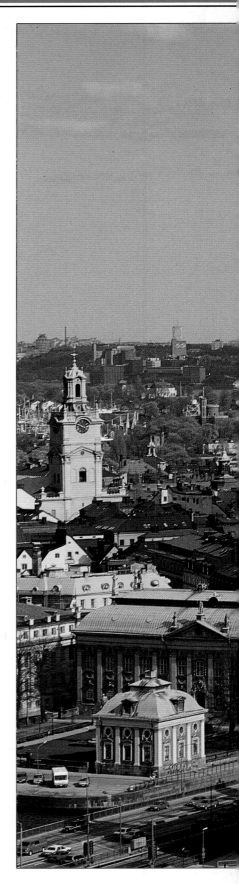

GAMLA STAN

Gamla Stan, the "old city" is the oldest district in Stockholm and the only one to have preserved intact many of the original facades from the seventeenth and eighteenth centuries.

The narrow, cobbled streets are lined with tiny restaurants, boutiques, antique shops (the most unusual of which sell ship's objects from dismantled vessels), craft shops, art galleries and pubs with live music, in a successful mixture of ancient and modern.

The tasteful reconstruction of period houses and the old-time atmosphere have made this one of the most popular districts with the Swedish intelligentsia.

It is very pleasant to stroll through the streets and squares of Gamla Stan, with the buildings seen along the way bringing you back in time through the different phases of Stockholm's history.

The Royal Palace, Kungliga Slottet, is an imposing Baroque building with many rooms and museums open to the public as well as the traditional "changing of the guard".

Stortorget is a good place to stop for coffee. It is the oldest square in the city and has fine merchant houses from the seventeenth century and stones commemorating the infamous bloodbath carried out by Christian of Denmark in 1520. St Nicolaos' Cathedral, the Storkyrkan, deserves a visit and has a beautiful wooden carving of "St George and the Dragon" by Bernt Notke of Lubeck.

A walk around Gamla Stan is not just a tourist itinerary but is above all fundamental to a full understanding of the history of Stockholm.

Top: A *view of Storkyrkan, the Cathedral of Stockholm*.
Below: S*ome glimpses of the Old City (Gamla Stan), in an excellent state of preservation*.

Right: *The splendid wooden statue of St George and the Dragon in the interior of the Storkyrkan.*
Below: *The Royal Palace (Kungliga Slottet).*

THE CITY HALL

What is it like to be a Nobel prize-winner for one night? You can experience this by dining in the Stadshuset, the restaurant situated in the cellars of the Town Hall, which offers all the different Nobel Prize menus from 1901 to the present day. But this is not the only attraction of one of the most important buildings in the city. Situated on the furthest point of the island of Kunsgholmen, the City Hall was built at the beginning of the century. It took 12 years to build and eight million red bricks were used in the construction.

The famous "Golden Room" is decorated with scenes from the history of Stockholm in gold mosaic, using 19 million pieces of mosaic. The Nobel Prize award ceremonies take place here in the imposing "Blue Room". From the high City Hall tower, on top of which the three crown symbol of Sweden stands tall, there is a magnificent view of the city and its canals.

Left: *In the Tower of the City Hall, there is an interesting Museum with works of art from various ages and places of origin.*
Below: *the typical outline of the City Hall, the tower of which is surmounted by a belfry and a gilded weathercock, bearing the three crowns of the national coat of arms.*
Right: *The Golden Room (Gyllene Salen) in the City Hall of Stockholm. The imposing mosaic at the far end of the chamber portrays the history of the city.*

Top: *The funeral monument to Birger Jarl, founder of the city.*
Below: *Two views of Stockholm, as seen from the Tower of the City Hall.*

Some images of the Parliament Building, with St George and the Dragon on the right.

Top: *The Stockholm Opera House, erected in 1890.*
Below: *One of the longest art galleries in the world: The City Metropolitan Gallery.*

Top: *Riddarholmen: the statue which commemorates Birger Jarl, and the Church of the Island of the Knights (Riddarholmskyrkan).*
Below: *The House of the Knights (Riddarhuset) with the statue of Gustav I Vasa.*

Some views of Kungsträdgården, formerly a garden reserved exclusively for the royal family. The statue which can be seen is that of Charles XII, a ruler who was greatly esteemed by many intellectuals of his age, well known for the wars.

THE VASA MUSEUM

On the 10 August 1628, on her maiden voyage, the Vasa, a great warship of the Swedish fleet, pride of the whole country and terror of the seas, sank after a journey of only 1300 metres. The Vasa was carrying aboard 64 cannons, hundreds of painted and gilded statues, masts 50 m high and a crew of one hundred.

The cause of the disaster is still unknown, but it is more than likely that it was due to the incomplete technical notions of the time.

The Vasa was built in the same way as other war vessels but was far bigger, higher and more heavily loaded with artillery than any earlier ship.

Some images of one of the most frequently-visited museums of Sweden. Recently, the Vasa Museum has been enriched by further valuable exhibits: these include some original sails from a boat, the oldest ever to have been found surviving intact.

The canons were recovered immediately but the entire ship was only brought to the surface 333 years later, thanks to the efforts and perseverance of the engineer Anders Franzen, one of the major experts on Swedish naval battles in the XVI and XVII centuries and in particular on ship- wrecked warships. Despite the long period under water, the Vasa was found in good condition, since the Baltic Sea does not have a high salt level.

Today, completely restored, the huge warship can be seen in all her splendour, complete with gilded decorations and impressive period fittings, in the "New Vasa Museum" on the island of Djurgården.

Inside the ultra modern museum, audiovisuals and guided visits in eight languages, retrace the history of the Vasa and Swedish shipping, bringing the visitor back to the adventurous era of warships in the XVII century.

The imposing hulk of the sailing-ship Vasa, *which remained submerged for more than three hundred years in the depths of the Baltic. The low salinity level of this sea has preserved the structure of the vessel from deterioration.* **Below:** *a detail of the decoration of the vessel.*

Students celebrating their degrees in front of the Nordiska Museet, on the island of Djurgården.

Top: *The Island of the Ships (Skeppsholmen): the nineteenth century ship Af Chapman, which is today the unusual site of a youth hostel.*
Below: *An external view of the Modern Art Museum (Moderna Museet).*

The most important art collection in Sweden is found in the National Museum. Page opposite: the sculpture "Wings", a work by Carl Milles, on the Blasieholmen Pier.

SKANSEN

The Skansen is the oldest open-air Museum in the world. It includes more than 150 ancient private and public buildings, originating in different parts of the country. The Museum began life with an idea by an ethnologist who wanted to illustrate the uses and customs of the various regions of Sweden to the citizens of Stockholm.

A number of popular feasts at various times of the year provide almost daily events in this museum, much-visited both by locals and tourists.

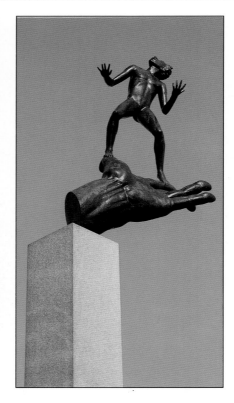

Some of the very well-known sculptures of Carl Milles are displayed in the gardens of his museum-home on the island of Lidingö.
Above, left: *the statue of Poseidon, (Neptune) which is also the subject of a famous fountain in the centre of Göteborg.*

THE SURROUNDING AREA OF STOCKHOLM

MILLESGÅRDEN

To the northeast of Stockholm, linked to the mainland by a bridge, lies the island of Lidingö, home to the spectacular and highly original museum dedicated to the Swedish sculptor, Carl Milles (1875-1955). Surrounded by parkland and occupying the former home and workshop of the artist, the museum is a rare example of the perfect balance between nature and art. The many sculptures and fountains created by Carl Milles are exquisitely displayed in a series of rooms and panoramic terraces. Many are copies of works on display in other countries, particularly in the United States, where Milles lived for several years, acquiring considerable fame. This takes nothing from the charm of the various statues which include the group of small threadlike figures of "angels playing music" suspended on high columns, the severe "Hand of God" or the merry mythological characters of the "Aganippe Fountain" on "Olga's Terrace", dedicated to the sculptor's beloved wife. She was also an artist and has left us a very fine portrait of her husband. Inside the museum Milles' rich personal collection is also on display. This numbers about 200 pieces and includes Greek and Roman art as well as other items from different countries and periods. The museum and gardens are open all year round.

DROTTNINGHOLM

Sweden also has a "Versailles".
This is the Drottningholm Palace, situated on the island of Lovön in Lake Mälaren, and since 1981, permanent residence of the royal family. Originally built in 1500, it was burnt to the ground and the present palace is in French Baroque style, as is the park, and dates from the end of the seventeenth century. It was Edwige Eleonor, wife of Carl X, who commissioned the building from the architects Nicodemus Tessin the Elder and Nicodemus Tessin the Younger. An English garden was built around the old park at the end of the eighteenth century. At the same time, a Chinese Pavilion and a Theatre, which has preserved its original decoration to this day, were built in the old park. It is perhaps the only theatre in the world that, in 200 years, has not altered in any way the original stage machinery, backdrops and interior

decoration. This is why Unesco in 1992 declared the Drottningholm Theatre, as well as the Palace and Chinese Pavilion to be a "World Heritage Site", a title only awarded to very few places and buildings of particular importance in the story of humanity.

THE ARCHIPELAGO

The 24,000 islands which make up the Stockholm Archipelago are known as the Skargården, "the garden on the rocks", and are a favourite holiday destination for the city's inhabitants.

Easily reached by ferry or taxiboat, but also by land, the islands, large and small, immediately reveal their brilliant colours and rich varied vegetation.

Their little towns are strikingly beautiful and have attracted artists and writers throughout the centuries.

August Strindberg spent his holidays in Dalarö, for example, and Carl Larsson and Anders Zorn have captured on canvas, with great intensity, the light and atmosphere of these islands, Once Stockholm's defensive outposts protecting the city from enemy invasion by sea, some of these islands preserve traces of their former function.

A sixteenth century fortress still stands in Vaxholm, one of the most popular towns in the Archipelago. This has now been transformed into a museum illustrating the history of Swedish military defence.

However, the greatest attraction of Vaxholm, besides the beautiful beaches and sporting facilities, are the old wooden houses.

The fretwork decorating attics, verandas, staircases and windows is extremely picturesque and attractive

One Swedish family in three owns a boat; thus it is easy to get to one's second house in one of the islands of the archipelago by this popular means of transport, or devote one's leisure time and energies to fishing and sailing. These are in fact some of the favourite occupations of those who visit this archipelago: with its 24,000 islands, covered with vegetation of all kinds, sometimes low-standing and variegated, and sometimes woody and rich in mushrooms, blueberries and wild strawberries: it is a real paradise for nature- and sea-lovers.

CENTRAL SWEDEN

The geographic centre of Sweden is also the true "heart" of the country, where, throughout the centuries, folk traditions have been kept alive and local people have great respect for their history. This is the province of Dalarna, breathtaking beautiful, and of great cultural and ethnographic interest. Especially around Lake Siljan, popular traditions have been strongly maintained.

On feastdays people dress in regional costume, play traditional music and participate in delightful folk ceremonies, such as the "church boats" which bring the faithful to Mass in the month of July.

However, the true character of the region is revealed in all its different facets during the Feast of St John, or Midsummer, which falls on the Saturday closest to the 24 June. Maypoles are set up all over the area and nobody goes to bed until the whole night has been spent dancing, singing and feasting.

Among the small towns on the shores of Lake Siljan some are of particular historic interest.

Mora is the birthplace of the famous Swedish painter Anders Zorn.

A museum has been dedicated to him but the town is also famous as the centre of an important historic event.

The Vasaloppet here, every March, thousands of cross-country skiers retrace the journey made by Gustav Vasa in 1521, when he travelled 88.8 km to convince the valley-dwellers to rise against the Danish king, Christian.

In Nusnäs, in particular, the visitor experiences sensations from days gone by. Here, for over a century, the Olsson family has been making the little wooden horses of Dalarna, a famous symbol of Sweden.

The wood for the horses comes from the forests around Lake Siljan and Lake Orsa.

The outline of the animals is machine made but the decoration is strictly hand-done.

After being painted red, blue or black, the little horses are decorated with designs inspired by wall frescoes found in the area.

The heart of the country lies in the province of Dalarna, the symbol of which is the typical red wooden pony.

Lake Siljan is one of the most popular tourist resorts in the summer. Several interesting events linked to popular tradition are held there each Summer, such as the boat regatta. It is possible to sail on the lake, and boats leave regularly for delightful trips around its shorts.

THE FABLES OF FATHER CHRISTMAS

Jultomte, the Swedish Father Christmas, spends the better part of the year in the heart of Dalarna, among frozen lakes in a great snow-covered park, at Tomteland. Here with his countless helpers, the gnomes, he deals with the thousands of requests for presents which arrive trustingly from all over the world. In front of his charming little wooden house is the majestic sleigh with the reindeer which draw it, on Christmas Eve, to the homes of thousands of children who are waiting for their presents. The interior of Father Christmas' house is a kind of dream: a great fireplace blazing in the sitting-room; a bed with a canopy in the form of a rainbow and a study crammed with books, presents and little letters which reach him from all over the world. On the upstairs floor, in a room which only little children who come to pay him a visit can enter, Jultomte tells wonderful stories, in an atmosphere of complete enchantment. Would you like to pay him a visit, or write him a letter? This is the address:
TOMTELAND,
Gesunda,
79043 Sollerön,
Sweden.

A *glimpse of the lively town of Mora.* Below: *the garden of the house of Anders Zorn, one of Sweden's greatest painters.* Opposite: *the monument to Gustav I Vasa.*

The wooden pony of Dalarna, painted in red and hand-decorated, has been the national symbol of Sweden since 1939. Even today, all these ponies are hand-made and only produced in the region of Dalarna.

In the workshops near the city of Mora, open to the public, it is possible to follow the various stages of manufacture at close quarters, but one can also learn to inlay or paint one's own pony.

IN THE STEPS OF GUSTAV VASA: THE VASALOPPET

The most popular ski competition held in Sweden is the **Vasaloppet**. This is a race of about 90 km, from Berga to Mora, in which men and women from any country can compete.

It is held every year to commemorate the patriotic action which Gustav Vasa performed in 1521 in the region of Dalarna.

He wanted to convince the Valley people to fight against the Danish King, Christian, but they were resistent to his advice, and initially refused to give him their support.

Gustav Vasa therefore headed on skis towards the Norwegian frontier, to pursue from there his exhortations to the national rebellion, but on his journey he was met by two men who begged him to turn back. These messengers had been sent by the citizens of Mora, who in the meantime had become convinced of the rightness of his intentions. His route to the city of Mora was more or less the one on which the Vasaloppet is run even today. Thousands of skiers take part in the competition on the first Sunday in March every year. It was organised for the first time in 1922 by the journalist, Anders Pers, and in that first event 119 skiers took part. Now, enrolment almost always exceeds 12000 competitors.

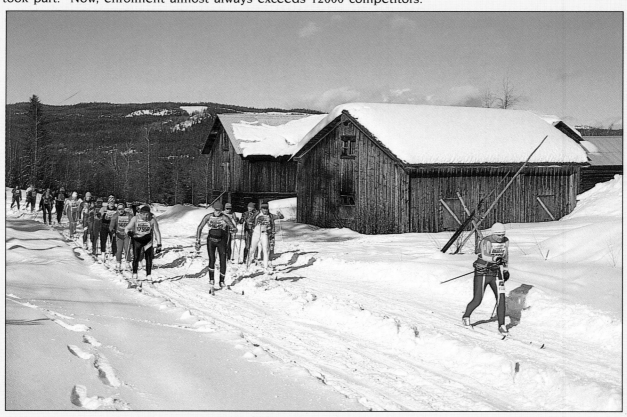

UPPSALA

When, on the Feast of Valpurga, on the 30 April, thousands of students mill gaily through the streets wearing the traditional little white cap, it is hard to believe that they study in the oldest University in Sweden, founded in Uppsala in 1477 and now a national monument.

The city, which is divided into a modern district and an old part, the "Gamla Uppsala", was an important political and religious centre from way back in Viking times, and the fine cathedral dating from the XIII century (but only consecrated in 1435) is still the seat of the archbishopric of Sweden.

It was also in Uppsala that the introduction of Lutheranism was determined in 1453.

The city of Uppsala has a past of great importance, both in religious and cultural terms. It is in fact considered Sweden's most "intellectual" city.

AN OLD LOVE AFFAIR WITH NATURE: CARL VON LINNÉ

Whatever we like to call him, Carl Nilsson, Carl von Linné, Carolus Linnaeus or just simply Linnaeus: if it is true that for the Swedes a beloved son has many names, this son of Sweden certainly has a special place in the hearts of his compatriots.

In fact, Linnaeus is undoubtedly one of the figures who brought greatest distinction to Swedish and international science in the eighteenth century, with his inspired studies of plants and living organisms. His love of travel and of the careful observation of all the elements of creation, his sensitivity towards the natural cycles, make him even today a point of reference for the everyday life of the Swedes.

His tract "*Systemae naturae*", the first edition of which dates from 1735, was the product of a careful and systematic study of the whole living world, based on rules of observation and denomination, through which the scientist succeeded in classifying the three realms of nature. In Uppsala, where Linnaeus was professor of medicine and botany, there are many places where his name is remembered. At No.27 of Svartbäcksgatan, there is a house where he lived for 35 years with his family; it has now been converted into a museum. Here one can still find the botanical gardens which he himself replanned in 1745, and which today house about 1300 floral species.

In the majestic cathedral of Uppsala, which dates from 1287, St. Eric, King and Patron Saint of Sweden is buried. Other great Swedes, such as Gustav Vasa and Linnaeus are also buried there.

LAKE MÄLAREN AND SIGTUNA

Lake Mälaren is a great lagoon basin, fed by a number of rivers which all converge on it. It is the third largest lake in Sweden, and its waters reach to the edges of Stockholm. Its broken contours, the thousands of deep inlets, the hundreds of islets, make it a place not to be missed for all tourists. On the island of **Birka** (B*jörkö*) in the ninth century, the evangelisation of the population who lived in this area began, undertaken by a French monk.

A witness to the importance of this place from a spiritual point of view is the interesting city of **Sigtuna**, founded by the first King of Sweden, Olaf Skötkonung, and first capital of the kingdom. It stands on the shores of Lake Mälaren, and ever since the middle ages has been an important point of reference for the christian faith. It was easily reached by boat, for in ancient times access was directly from the Baltic Sea, of which Lake Mälaren was then a deep inlet. It still has important evidence of its historic role; among them several stone churches of the 12th century, ruins of ancient monasteries, and fine wooden houses, as well as a **Town Hall**, built in the typical local style.

There are many ruins of the numerous mediaeval churches: among these, the **Church of St Olof** and the Dominican Church of **Santa Maria klosterskyrkan**, dating from the 13th century.

A view of Lake Mälaren and the cross of Ansgar, a witness to the ancient spiritual character of this area.

Some views of Birka, the first city founded in Sweden. It was in this area that the French monk, Ansgar, to whom the chapel in the top photoraph is dedicated, began the evangelisation of the country.

ÖREBRO

Örebro, a city of fundamental importance in the history of Sweden, is the capital of the small province of Närke, to the south of Dalarna. Many sovereigns have stayed in Örebro Castle, originally a lookout tower erected by Birger Jarl in 1200. During the Danish occupation in the XV century, the castle was refuge to many heroes of Swedish independence. In every century Örebro was the seat of important resolutions. In 1347 Parliament ratified the first common law here, in 1436 the city became the seat of the Estates General, in 1522 Gustav Vasa's troops took the city and seven years later the Lutheran Reform was voted in. In 1617 the first Parliamentary rules were passed and finally, in 1810, right here in Örebro, the French marshal Jean Baptiste Bernadotte, founder of the present reigning dynasty, was designated hereditary prince, Carl XIV, of Sweden. Despite repeated restorations, the castle has preserved its sixteenth century appearance.

Also of interest is the "Swampen", the mushroom, a modern tower 58m high which has become a symbol of the city.

The small town of Örebro, on Lake Hjälmaren. Not far from the castle-fortress, there are two unusual Museums, one dedicated to footwear and the other to cookery.

At Sundborn Carl Larsson often found the source of inspiration for his paintings.
Photo below: *a self-portrait of the artist,* **and opposite:** *his beautiful house in the green countryside.*

SUNDBORN: THE WATERCOLOURS OF CARL LARSSON

The warm, magical atmosphere of Nordic homes, with wooden window frames and floors, ceramic stoves, pastel colours and the presence of chubby fair-haired children, has been portrayed with great affection and empathy, as well as with extraordinary talent by the Swedish painter Carl Larsson (1853-1919). His water-colours, copies of which have travelled all over the world, are on display in the Sundborn museum in Dalarna, once the painter's favourite home.

Pretty as a doll's house, brightly coloured and welcoming, "Lilla Hyttnas" was given to Carl Larsson by his father-in-law. It was here that the artist came to live, with his wife, on his return from a lengthy period of study in other parts of Europe. In France he had come into contact with the Impressionists and had embraced the technique of painting outdoors and the use of water-colour.

Back in Sweden he championed these techniques against those of official painting, supported by the Academy, and devoted himself almost exclusively to the celebration of historic and patriotic subjects.

In Dalarna, Larsson discovered his original gift for depicting familiar, intimate subjects, homely interiors and ordinary moments of daily life as well as landscapes and simple country scenes.

The sunniest and most joyful aspect of Swedish nature is revealed in these paintings in all their tender magic.

THE SOUTH OF SWEDEN

An unspoilt landscape, stretching over sandy beaches, small lakes and rivers, ideal for fishing and canoing: a great plain which has won the title of "Granary of Sweden" for this area; luxuriant forests - all this and more can be found in the southernmost part of Sweden, known as **Skåne**. This is one of the more highly populated regions, and it contains much evidence of the past, such as the Church of Dalby, dating from 1030, the first religious building to be constructed in stone, or the frescoes of the Roman era in the great church of Vä, near Kristianstad. But relics of the past go even further back in time: from the Bronze Age there are the A*les Stenar*, (the Stones of Ale), near **Ystad**, an evocative and mysterious stone circle of *menhirs*, similar to those of Stonehenge in England.

Among cities which should not be missed is **Lund**, which has just celebrated its thousandth anniversary; a lively university city with a fine cathedral and a fourteenth century astronomical clock, or **Malmö**, the third city of the country and a very important port. In the province of Skåne, the sea is never more than fifty kilometres away, and bathing resorts are numerous and very popular. Among these are the mediaeval **Skanör and Falsterbo**. The coast, consisting of fine sandy beaches, becomes more rocky and indented towards the north east, near **Karlskrona**, built on about thirty islets linked by bridges. Further to the north, one enters **Småland**, where the forests become even thicker, and the first conifers are found.

This is the kingdom of glassmaking, between the cities of **Kalmar**, the provincial capital, and **Växjö**.

Kalmar has an interesting cathedral, covered with bronze, and its ancient fortress was for a long time the frontier with Denmark, when the Danes governed the south.

The typical countryside of the south of Sweden.

The bridge connecting the city with the island of Öland, inaugurated in 1972, is the longest bridge in Europe - 6072 metres in all. The beautiful islands of **Öland** and **Gotland** complete the panorama of beauty which this region has to offer. Inhabited since the Bronze Age, they have Viking remains, stone-carved figures and tombs in the form of a ship, as well as unforgettable natural scenery.

One of the most popular traditions of the region of Skåne is the grand supper of St Martin, which is held on 10th November, the eve of the saint's feast. The leading role in this feast is undoubtedly played by the goose, bred in the great wide fields of the southern farms. The partnership between the goose and the saint goes back at least as far as 1567, as we find confirmed by a document found in the region of Stockholm, in which the goose is specifically associated with St Martin's Day. But the Grand Supper of St Martin is a typical custom of this region of the south, and it also provides an opportunity to taste elaborate and unusual dishes, such as the spettaka, a typical local dessert, one metre high.

MALMÖ

The third city in Sweden and second biggest port in the country, Malmö faces southwards and is regularly linked with Copenhagen.

An important centre in the Hanseatic League and a military stronghold, the city passed from Denmark to Sweden only towards the end of the XVII century when the Peace of Roskilde definitively ratified Swedish possession. Although a business and industrial city, Malmö has retained a southern atmosphere, gay and carefree, with many bars, restaurants, little shops and narrow streets with intense commercial activity.

It is still a very green city with many parks, including the large Limhamn park where there are extensive sporting facilities.

There is an echo of the past around Lilla Torget, a small square paved with the original large square stones and lined with half-timbered houses from the XVII and XVIII centuries. Malmö is also home to one of the largest theatres in Scandinavia, the Stadsteatern, which was founded in 1944 and has a capacity of 1700 spectators.

LUND

For centuries the imposing profile of Lund cathedral, in the verdant province of Skåne, has welcomed travellers as they neared the city.

Founded in 1080 by the Danish king Canute, the Saint, and consecrated in 1145, Lund cathedral is definitely the oldest archbishopric in Scandinavia and one of the finest Romanesque buildings in northern Europe.

As well as the crypt, which contains the tombs of many illustrious Swedes, the choir stalls in carved wood and the altar, the astronomical clock dating from the XIV century is of great interest.

Every afternoon at half past three, the clock reveals its fascinating mechanism, horsemen challenge each other in a duel, musicians play their trumpets, the organ plays "in dulci jubilo" and tiny doors open to welcome three miniature Wise Men, lining up to pay their tribute to Our Lady and the Child.

Lund is a very attractive town, with narrow picturesque streets, the old market and the Lundagard park where the royal residence from the XVI century, built in red brick, was transformed into a University in 1666.

Today it is still the library of the present university, second in importance only to the Uppsala library.

Lund is a particularly lively and animated town, thanks to the 30,000 students who attend the University, especially during the Valpurga Feast on the 30 April and the Mid-May Carnival which takes place every four years.

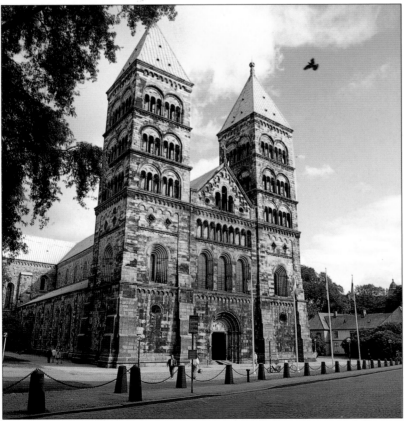

The cheerful southern city of Lund has just celebrated its thousandth anniversary.

HELSINGBORG

For many tourists, Helsingborg is their first encounter with Sweden. Anyone arriving in Sweden from Denmark in fact, leaves behind Hamlet's castle in the town of Helsingør and boards one of the many ferry-boats covering the 4.5 km of sea which separates the two countries.

An important European capital in the seventeenth century, Helsingborg was disputed for a long time by Denmark and Sweden, given its privileged position dominating the Baltic Sea.

Today, it is above all an industrial city which preserves important ruins from the past, such as the Karnan Tower and the fine Church of St Mary, the Sankta Maria Kyrkan.

The Church itself is in the Gothic style and built simply in brick, but it is the interior of the church with its detailed decoration that is of great artistic interest.

The pulpit, baptismal font, candlesticks, stained windows and in particular, the altarpiece by the German school of the XV century, are extremely beautiful and merit a visit.

Two views of the ancient capital of Scandinavia, Helsingborg.

THE ISLAND OF GOTLAND

Gotland, the "good land" is the largest island in the Baltic sea, a jewel of limestone rock and favourite destination (along with the small nearby island of Farö) for artists and politicians, thanks to its beautiful sandy beaches and rich exotic vegetation.

The temperate climate favours a luxurious flora and the island has extensive deciduous forests and countless varieties of flowers, including 36 species of orchids. However, Gotland is above all a real ornithologist's paradise with one of the richest varieties of birds in Europe, There are 157 species of birds nesting here, which become 350 in the springtime.

The protection of this important natural heritage is carried out by the 40 government-run nature reserves present on the island.

Formerly a Viking town, then one of the most powerful seats of the Hanseatic League, Gotland's importance over the centuries is well documented in numerous ruins and archaeological remains from different eras.

Stone tumuli from the Bronze Age, ship-shaped Viking tombs, churches and Mediaeval fortifications are found all over the island. The most significant remains from this period are to be found in Visby, the capital of Gotland, known as the "city of ruins and roses".

The original walls from the XIII-XIV centuries are still standing, with a communication trench 3 km long, pierced by 38 of the original 44 towers and by 18 gates.

The small civic museum "Gotland Fornsal" is of great historic and artistic interest for the high quality of its prehistoric, Viking and Mediaeval exhibits.

Visby is a very picturesque Mediaeval city with many churches. Some of these are in ruins but fortunately not the fine Cathedral of St Mary in Romanesque-Gothic style.

The ruins of the church of St Nicholas are used as a backdrop for the sacred Mediaeval play "Petrus of Dacia" by F. Mehler, which is put on every summer during the "Visby Festival". In the first week of August every year, the clock is turned back and the city becomes Mediaeval again. Local people dress in period costume and the visitor rubs shoulders with knights, merchants, noblewomen, witches and acrobats in the crowded streets.

A jousting tournament and a historic pageant conclude the week's festivities.

The island of Gotland has been described as the "mediaeval garden of the Baltic". It preserves vestiges of nearly ten thousand years of history, and in August, the island capital of Visby relives its past for a whole week. The city still has thirty-eight of its original towers, and eighteen gates placed between the bastions, as well as its old streets with houses from many epochs. UNESCO has included it in the list of world heritage sites, because of its unique cultural and historical patrimony.

THE VIKINGS

The era of the Vikings in Sweden (800 - 1050 Christian Era) was characterised by great expansionist movements eastward, with the aim of exchanging merchandise and sacking the territories along the Baltic Coast, and the banks of the rivers which now flow through the Russian plain.

Setting out in manoeuvrable, lightweight craft, the Viking expeditions from the ninth century onward created strategic centres from the commercial point of view, like Rurik, for example, which takes its name from one of their chiefs. It was in fact from this name that the vast plain was called Russia, and in it the Vikings created the principalities of Novgorod and Kiev.

They pushed as far as the Black Sea and

even the Caspian Sea, where they set up commercial links with the Byzantine Empire and the Arab world.

A significant testimony to the period is provided by the Bildstenar, massive stone figures, decorated with inscriptions in runic characters, intended to commemorate some battle or illustrious personality, or to give thanks to the gods.

In the isle of Gotland, there are a large number of stone carvings, characterised by decoration which is predominantly geometric, and which gradually becomes more and more complex, with inscriptions in spiral form and with the first zoomorphic representations.

These latter developed later on into the so-called "Vendel" style.

In Uppland quite elaborate carved stones can be seen, with interwoven decoration dating back to the last Viking migrations, around the 11th century.

In this period there was also a high level of quality, to be seen in the items of jewellery found in certain of the Viking tombs.

There are more than 400 windmills on the island of Öland, and they are protected as a national monument. The landscape of the island with its low-lying multicoloured vegetation and its fine sun-baked beaches has led the royal family to choose it as their summer vacation resort.

THE ISLAND OF ÖLAND

Some remember Öland as the kingdom of the wind and some cannot forget its beautiful sunny beaches, dramatic sunsets and infinite horizons.

The royal family spends summer holidays in the Solliden villa on this charming island.

Linked to the historic town of Kalmar by the longest bridge in Europe (6072 m), the island is 135 km in length and only 15 km in breadth at its widest point.

Rich in history, the island has many Viking runic stones and also some remains from the Iron Age.

The village of Eketorpet, an archaeological site dating back to the V century BC, is of particular interest.

Careful restoration of the original structure has made it possible for the visitor to understand many aspects of life at that time.

Many of the island's churches date back to the Middle Ages. However, the most striking feature of the island is the presence of more than 400 windmills, designated as national monuments.

The only road running the whole length of the island from north to south crosses the "Stora Alvaret", the Great Heath - a flat stretch with no trees. Various species of flowers and the passage of countless migratory birds provide great interest for botanists and ornithologists.

From the Lange Jan lighthouse on the southernmost point of the island there is a wonderfully romantic view at sunset

KOSTA

Archaeological finds from 2000 BC reveal that the Egyptians already knew how to make glass.

Glass-making was introduced into Sweden around 1550, when Gustav Vasa invited a Venetian glass-blower to the Stockholm court. The first Swedish workshop however was opened in Kosta, in the heart of the "Glass Country", in 1742. This is still one of the most famous names in Swedish glassmaking.

VÄXJÖ

Shining and tinkling on tables all over the world, Småland crystal delights guests with its elegant lines and pure transparency.

Småland is a province in southern Sweden which boasts very old glassworks, whose hallmarks such as "Kosta", "Boda" or "Orrefors", just to name a few, are famous all over the world The "Glass Country" is situated between the city of Kalmar and Växjö, in an area covered in forests that, from 1700 onwards, provided an important source of fuel for the furnaces. Today more than 17 glassworks produce a range of original pieces and the visitor can see all the phases of the working of the glass and buy crystal for less than in the shops.

In the city of Växjö, the "Småland Museum" illustrates the complete history of this craft through the ages.

More than 27,000 pieces of glassware are on display in the museum. These document the evolution of the art of glassmaking and the different styles proposed by designers over the centuries.

VIMMERBY

Children all over the world have longed, at one time or another, to enter into the enchanted world of their favourite books and meet the characters they know so well.

In Sweden this is possible.

Vimmerby, a small Mediaeval town in the province of Småland, is the birthplace of one of the world's most important children's writers – Astrid Lindgren. A few kilometres northeast of the city, the "world of Astrid Lindgren", source of enchantment for countless children, has been recreated in a miniature village with surroundings, buildings and characters from her most famous books.

Children can go in and out of the houses of "Ronya", "Rasmus" and "My little Me", meet "Pippi Longstocking" and go riding with the "Brothers Lionheart" or play with the hens, sheep and pigs of "Emil", experiencing the joy of being, at least for a day, the protagonists of their best loved books.

KALMAR

Kalmar is the capital of the Småland region. Its cathedral is coated with bronze, and its fine ancient fortress, rebuilt during the Renaissance, was once the frontier-post of Sweden when the southern part of the country was under Danish rule. The bridge which links the city to the island of Öland is the longest in Europe, 6072 metres in all.

SOUTH-WESTERN SWEDEN

Amid hundreds of enchanted lakes and forests, south-western Sweden offers countless attractions to the tourist.

Among these is the **Bohuslän**, one of the most ancient inhabited areas of the land.

At **Tanum** there are dolmens, and rock inscriptions which go back to the Bronze Age, among the most interesting prehistoric remains in the whole country.

In the province of **Västergötland**, we find great lakes such as **Vänern** and **Vättern**, and an excellently preserved natural environment, in which a host of fabulous castles rise up, such as that of **Läckö**, or silent abbeys like the **Abbey of Varnhem**, a Cistercian monastery with buildings dating back to the second half of the 13th century.

Right in the middle of Lake Vänern is a magnificent **National Park, that of the Archipelago of Djurö**, whose area includes around 30 islets, coated with pinewoods and broken up by craggy outcrops. Here a rich variety of birdlife can be found nesting.

Not far away is another important protected zone; the **National Park of Tiveden**, whose magical landscape of age-old forests provides the background for many of Sweden's legends and fables.

In **Dalsland** and in the **Värmland**, it is possible to go on interesting and delightful excursions, either by boat or by bicycle among the rivers and lakes typical of the zone.

While following the paths which run alongside the clear streams, and which lead through landscapes of delicate beauty - small villages and corners of uncontaminated nature - it is easy to forget the worries of everyday life and plunge onself into a natural context absolutely made for the human dimension..

Picnicking on the shores of one of south-western Sweden's many lakes on a warm summer day, is one of the favourite activities of Swedish families.

THE RIGHT TO NATURE

A *house of the south-west region of Sweden, surrounded by a garden and lands which are preferably always cultivated. Sweden is one of the few countries which applies the "alleman-srätt", the right of all, which allows everyone, by an unwritten law, to walk freely through the natural countryside, and to cross the land of others provided no damage is caused. The only "private" areas are those in the immediate vicinity of the houses and summer dwellings, and naturally, the lands which are under cultivation.*

Trekking and golf are both very popular in Sweden. In the southern regions, there are countless opportunities to enjoy them. In Båstad, for instance, some famous golf tournaments take place on the fifty or so high-level courses which are found in the area.

Top: *The magic circle of menhirs, known as Ales Stenar, not far from Kåseberga. This circular complex of megaliths dates back to the Bronze Age,*
Below: *A view of the central square of the town of Ystad.*

KARLSKRONA

Karlskrona is the capital of the small province of Blekinge, and is the second port and primary naval base of Sweden. This elegant and aristocratic city stands on around thirty islands, linked by bridges. It possesses an interesting maritime Museum, well known for the original architecture.

GÖTEBORG

Like a narrow blue ribbon winding its way through the Swedish countryside, the Göta Kanal, constructed in the XIX century and navigable for its entire length of 518 km, connects Stockholm to Göteborg, Sweden's second biggest city and the most important port in Scandinavia. Founded in 1621 by king Gustav Adolphus, the city owes its town plan and canals to a group of Dutch architects.

Everywhere, however, there are traces of the city's maritime history. First and foremost is the East Indian Company, Östindiska Huset, founded in 1700 by Dutch, German and Scottish merchants and now

Göteborg, Sweden's second city. The city offers numerous attractions, including museums and exhibitions of antiques, parks and theatres, such as the Göteborgs Operan, perhaps the most modern and efficient building in the world dedicated to the theatre and operatic music.

transformed into a Historical, Archaeological and Ethnographical Museum.

Then there is the Maritime Museum, the Sjöfartsmuseet and the Feskekorka, the fish market, a lively place full of activity. The Poseidon Fountain, a work by Carl Milles, which stands in the Götaplatsen, the commercial heart of the city, is a homage to the wealth and majesty of the sea.

Although the sea and sailors are this elegant city's lifeblood, Göteborg is also very attentive to the arts and there is lively participation in a variety of artistic activities.

Worthy of mention are not only the excellent Museum of Fine Art, the Konstmuseet with a good collection of Italian, Spanish and Flemish art as well as works from the Swedish and French schools from the XVII to the XX century, and the Museum of Applied Arts, the Röhsska Konstslöjdmuseet, but also the Antikhallarna, the greatest antique market in all of Sweden.

For entertainment there are many theatres, cafes and bars, and especially Liseberg, an amusement park with a thousand different attractions.

On this page, *several glimpses of the city of Göteborg: the fountain of Poseidon, the exterior of the Museum of Fine Arts, and one of its exhibition rooms. Opposite: an idea of the city can be gained by roaming around its canals on board the "Paddan", the boat which does the rounds between the various parts of the city.* **In the upper photo,** *the city's Cathedral and the statue of the sovereign who founded Göteborg, Gustavus Adolphus II.*

TANUM

Arriving in Sweden from southern Norway, Bohuslän province is the first one you meet. This is an area with an ancient civilisation and many archaeological traces of the Bronze Age and Viking period. However, the historic and cultural value of the region is matched by its marvellous scenery – a magnificent indented coastline, scores of islands and great expanses of heather.

Tanum, an archaeological site of exceptional interest, is situated in this region. Here, rock carvings dating back to 3000 years ago are still perfectly preserved.

Carved with stone implements in the grey granite which is typical of this region, these ancient images illustrate many aspects of life and society at that time. Originally they were probably coloured brown and ochre and some sort of grease was used to keep the colour fast, today a red line traced on the carvings helps the visitor to pick out the different images represented.

Many of the scenes depict boats, human beings (the women are recognisable with their long hair and the men with their extremely obvious sexual parts), animals of different types and hunting scenes.

In Tanum there are innumerable dolmens, and the finest and most elaborate rock-carvings in the whole of Sweden.

Some of the splendid rock carvings of Tanum, representing scenes of hunting and fishing as well as everyday life.

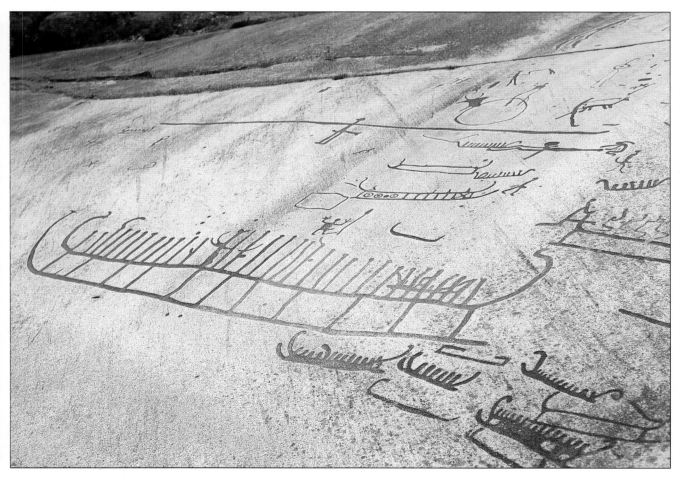

In the province of Västergötland, near Lake Vänern, the magnificent castle of Läckö stands on a promontory. The castle has around 148 rooms, restored in the seventeenth century.

Not far from Läckö is the abbey of Varnhem, one of the most ancient of Cistercian monasteries. Within its walls there is a church dating from 1260.

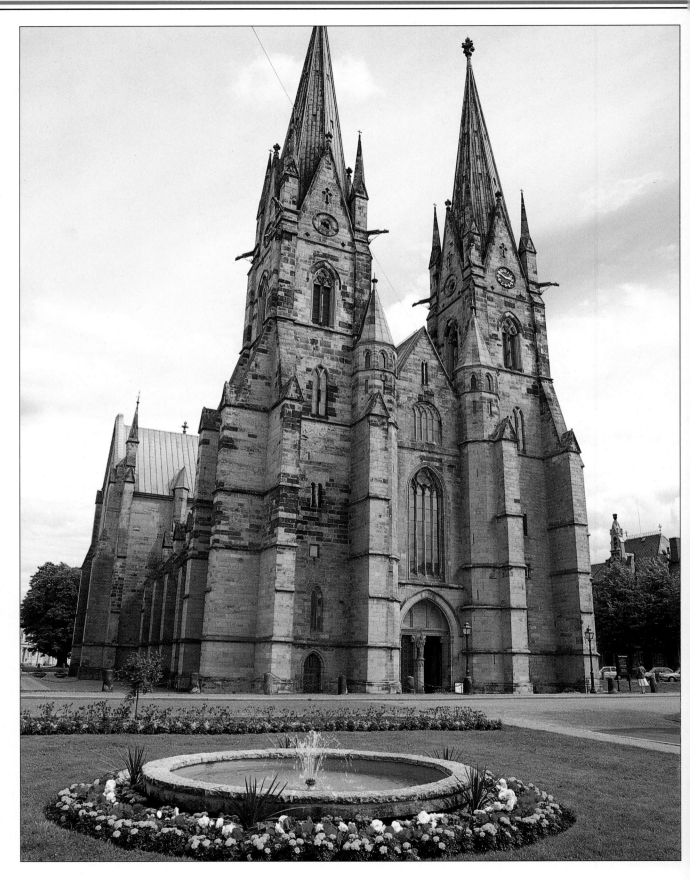

On this page, some images of the great Lake Vättern. On the side, the imposing cathedral of Skara.

VADSTENA

The town of Vadstena stands on the eastern shore of Lake Vättern, in Östergötland, and it was built around an **Abbey** dedicated to **St Bridget**, dating from the 14th century.

Inside the Abbey walls there is the "blue church" (*Blåkyrkan*), so-called because of the pale blue stones of which it is built. It is a Gothic building of great elegance, with three naves, and it contains important paintings and sculptures of the Lubeck School, among which is the tomb of the saint.

Not far away from here, is the most ancient evidence of writing in Sweden. This is the runic stone of **Rök**, on which is written a very ancient text, in absolute terms the earliest in all Swedish literature.

Another great attraction of this picturesque city is the **Vadstena slott**, the imposing castle in the Dutch style, dating from the period of the Swedish Renaissance. It was the residence of Gustav Vasa, who ordered it to be built as a city-fortress in 1545. At present it houses one of the State Archives.

On the main street and square of the town there are buildings of historical and artistic interest, such as the 15th century **Town Hall**, the **City Museum** and towards the Abbey, the **Gamla teatern**, the old wooden theatre.

The castle of Vadstena on Lake Vättern and the statue of St Bridget inside the church dedicated to her. On the opposite page, above, the Altar of the Rosary, and below, a painting by Van Dyck and a portrait of Gustav I Vasa in the rooms of the Castle.

JÖNKÖPING: THE FAMOUS SWEDISH MATCHES

World-renowned Swedish matches have been produced here in Jönköping since 1840.

The phases involved in the creation of what is now an item of daily use are illustrated in the "Match Museum" in this town near Lake Vättern.

Set in the former factory of the brothers Carl Frans and Johan Edvard Lundstrom, the first to produce matches on an industrial scale, the museum retraces the history of this common but extremely useful household object.

Originally the subject of elaborate chemical studies until the

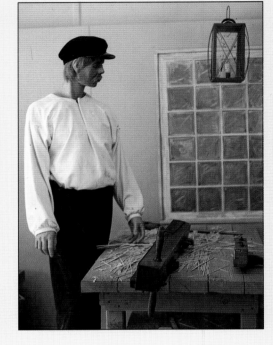

so-called **"safety match"** was invented, match production became one of the major forces in the Swedish economy.

Even today the 14,000 matchbox labels made in Jönköping and printed with a variety of different images and colours are collector's items. The museum is only one of the attractions of this ancient city which is also seat of the Court of Appeal for southern Sweden. Jönköping has retained interesting buildings from the seventeenth century and can boast one of the most beautiful beaches on Lake Vättern, right within the city.

NORTHERN SWEDEN

The majestic vastness of the northern regions of Sweden, the silence in which they are wrapped, and the rarefied light which illuminates them, are an unforgettable experience for the visitor. Here the beech and pinewood forests gradually give way to moss and lichen, the final representatives of a flora which must eventually surrender to the ice and freezing conditions of a winter that can last as long as nine months. The northern landscape is made up of snowy peaks, great lakes, frozen all year round, endless forests, stretches covered with moss, vast moors, canyons and valleys where the bear and the musk ox live undisturbed, together with countless species of birds. This is the best preserved natural environment in Europe; in these places, man has lived since prehistory.

There are hundreds of rock inscriptions to prove this, for example those in Jämtland and in Ångermanland, which represent animals, boats and people in movement, all drawn with astonishing precision.
One of the largest open-air museums in Sweden is at **Jamtli**, where an attempt is made to recreate the atmosphere of daily life in the 18th and 19th centuries by means of about forty farms which have been specially equipped for the purposes Naturally, national parks and protected areas are not lacking: in the province of Härjedalen there is the **National Park of Sonfjället**, characterised by majestic forests and glaciers dating from the Ice Age. The most northerly park in Sweden is the **National Park of Vadvetjåkka**, in the area of which there are lakes and an innumerable

quantity of plants and rare birds, who find their ideal environment in the humid climate of the north Atlantic. Thousands of streams rush helter-skelter through this enchanted landscape; among them is the Pite Älv, the greatest non-navigable mountain stream in Europe. Here we can admire the impressive **Waterfall of Storforsen**, about 80 metres (260 feet) high, which hurls itself into the waters of the lakes below along a stretch of five kilometres. And then there are thousands of small towns, isolated centres of habitation, picturesque fishing villages, like those which are to be found along the High Coast, to the north of Sundsvali, at **Nordingrå**, or those of the island of **Ulvö**. Surely a thrilling adventure in the summer, beneath a sun which shines almost continuously.

The sun lights up a group of houses in northern Sweden. In the winter, in the northern zone, the sun never rises above the horizon, and the only light comes from the very long dawn of the Aurora Borealis, a unique and memorable phenomenon of these latitudes.

HOTEL BELOW ZERO: THE ARCTIC HALL

Near the city of Kiruna, the main centre of Swedish Lapland, in the village of Jukkasjärvi, every year a hotel is built entirely out of ice and snow. Its name is **Arctic Hall**, and it is a product of the fertile imagination of Ingve Bergqvist, who is in charge of the tourist village of Jukkasjärvi.

In 1991, the first building began, with 60 square metres of floorspace, using a basic aluminium structure, on to which the snow was pressed. Once the snow had frozen, the structure was dismantled, and a genuine, unreinforced snow-chamber survived. From year to year the building was made more and more complex, until in 1994, with the assistance of the architect, Aimo Räisänen, then it became an actual hotel, with restaurants, bars, a cinema with an ice screen, churches with an ice font, and an art gallery. The spacious bedrooms, all rigorously glacial, and decorated and sculptured with unadulterated transparent ice, are all provided with full modern comforts, including TV and stereophonic equipment, and they can house up to 60 persons.

The hotel is not equipped with central heating, and the internal temperature is constant at 2-3 degrees below zero, while outside it can descend to -35°; hence the clients come provided with thermic sportswear and padded sleepingbags, while the icebeds are covered with reindeer hides.

Naturally, in the Spring Arctic Hall disappears, and is then rebuilt in November, always in a different form from before.

LAPLAND

Swedish Lapland is a natural paradise of incredible beauty, enhanced by a variety of colours which change according to the season. A sportsman's kingdom, Swedish Lapland has a population of about 15,000 Same. There are 2,500 Same engaged in reindeer breeding and it is estimated that at present reindeer number about 250,000.

The biggest city in the region is **Luleå**, founded in 1621. The city's main attraction is the old centre, now situated 10 km from the present one: **"Gammelstad"**.

Here there is a church dating from the XV century, surrounded by more than 400 small wooden houses which form the parrochial village.

Further north, a visit to **Kiruna** is a must. This is an important town in the centre of a mining region. The unusual church, built in 1912, recalls the shape of the Lapp tents, known as *kåta*.

Those daring enough to attempt the ascent of Mount Kebneikaise, 100 km south of Kiruna, will be rewarded with a fascinating view of the midnight sun, shining tirelessly over the boundless Lapp silence.

Gammelstads Kyrkstad is now on **UNESCOS** list of World Inheritance. It is Sweden's largest and best preserved "Ky stad" and represents a more than 400 year old tradition. It has 425 small cottages and they were built for people w lived far away from the church.

ISTORICAL NOTES

story of Sweden starts about 00 BC when the thick layer of entirely covering the country an to melt and retreat northds leaving the southern regions overed.

as then that the first nomadic ters and fishermen began to ar- and only in the fourth milleni- were they followed by the first led peoples who lived together villages and engaged in agricul- and the rearing of livestock. splendid cave paintings show- hunting scenes and episodes n daily life, which are the earli- pictorial witnesses we have, e from the Bronze Age and are perfectly preserved today.

Roman historian Tacitus was fist writer to leave us informa- on Sweden's early inhabitants. his book "Germany", he de- bes the Swedish population as ng of Germanic origin – Goths in South and Svear in the area und Lake Mälaren.

as actually the Svear, defeating Goths, who gave the country its ne "Sverige", Sweden, and es- lished their religious and politi- capital at Uppsala.

vas Tacitus who first mentioned Lapps, or better Finns, who are scribed as a people living on the ors and in the forests "reaching where the land seems to end".

eden's isolation throughout the ceding centuries ended with the t of the Viking era (700-1000 . The Vikings were a sea-faring ple about whom we still know y little and whose very name is uded in mystery.

ent studies have shown that al- ugh the Vikings were bloody violent warriors, pirates and enturers, they developed etheless a great and complex lisation. Not only excellent sea- rs, the Vikings produced poets, sts and sophisticated explorers gave much to the different ples and civilisations in the ds they conquered.

ert Viking seamen, in their fast gboats known as "drakkar", ap-

parently used spar, a mineral which polarises the sun's light, to find their way at sea.

The most beautiful runic stones are kept in the museum in Visby, the capital of the island of Gotland. These stones are decorated with in- scriptions in the Viking alphabet and drawings representing events and characters in Nordic mythology and sagas.

Great Viking tumuli and ship- shaped tombs can be visited all over Sweden.

The Swedish Vikings, who settled mainly in the region around present-day Stockholm, put Sweden in contact with Russia, Constantinople, Great Britain and Ireland and opened new commer- cial routes.

As relations with Germany and England gradually intensified and missionaries were sent to Sweden, Christianity spread through the land. By the XII century it had become the dominant religion following the baptism of King Olaf Eriksson and the assignation of an Archbishop to Sweden.

At the same time the economic and political power of the country was consolidated with the annexation of Finland and the foundation of the capital, Stockholm.

In 1389, Margareta, Queen of Denmark and Norway, received the Swedish crown and the Scandina- vian kingdoms were united with the Union of Kalmar, a coalition formed to check the power of the Hanseatic League in Northern Germany.

However, different interests in the three Scandinavian countries provoked a series of insurrections and popular revolts.

The most violent episode of all was when Christian II of Denmark crushed the Swedish resistance in the so-called "bloodbath" of 1520.

Swedish independence was finally attained by Gustav Eriksson Vasa. He instigated an insurrection in Dalarna, succeeded in involving the whole country and put an end to Danish dominion and the Union of Kalmar.

At Mora in Dalarna, every year thou- sands of cross-country skiers still retrace the historic 88.8 km long route that Gustav Vasa took at the start of the revolution.

Gustav Vasa was elected sovereign ruler of Sweden and from then on the Swedish monarchy became hereditary. During the Vasa dy- nasty, which lasted 150 years, Protestantism was introduced into Sweden and Lutheranism became the dominant religion.

In the XVII century, during the reign of Gustav Adolphus II (1611-32), Sweden became the most powerful kingdom in Europe, conquering re- gions in Russia and Poland. The sol- diers in the king's army were for the most part peasants and practically the sole source of finance was the Falun mines, but Gustav Adolphus was a military genius and his ad- vanced strategies and tactics earned him enormous success. In 1648 the Peace of Westphalia rati- fied the Swedish territorial gains.

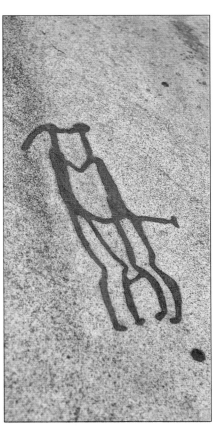

Gustav Adolphus was succeeded by his daughter Christina who was crowned, however, only in 1644. Queen Christina had a profound influence on the development of Swedish cultural life. During her Regency, Stockholm became an elegant and renowned capital. Artists and writers from all countries, in particular Germany, Holland and France, were guests at her court. The French philosopher Descartes died, in fact, in Stockholm, where he was staying as a guest of the Queen. In 1654, Christina converted to Catholicism, abandoned Sweden and settled in Rome where she continued her policy of encouraging artistic activities. The famous Arcadian Academy was, in fact, founded in her palace in Rome. The enormous magnolia tree where Christina of Sweden used to read or rest in the shade, can still be seen today in Rome, in front of the Botanical Gardens. During the reigns of Christina's successors, Sweden succeeded in recovering Scania and the southern provinces from Denmark, as well as Baltic and German regions,

and founded her first colonies. This period of enormous power ended with the death of Carl XII (1718), a strong personality defeated by Peter the Great at Poltava. The country lost many of her possessions and her political and economic position was weakened. It was then that the ruling class took the situation in hand, limiting the powers of the king and giving control to a Council of State responding to a Parliament (Riksdag), made up of the members of two parties, Liberals and Conservatives. The accession to the throne of Gustav III, nephew of Frederick the Great of Prussia, marked a new revival of the power of the monarchy, a veritable "enlightened despotism". Patron of the arts and a great admirer of French architecture and sculpture, Gustav III encouraged artistic activity, which was stimulated and sustained by the foundation of the Swedish Academy. Among the modern, far-sighted reforms instituted by Gustav III it is worth mentioning religious freedom, the possibility for members of all social

classes to hold public office, abolition of torture and the f dom of the press. The King was sassinated by a nobleman, his cessors were not as able and S den suffered a period of dec until the French marshal Jean tiste Bernadotte was crowned Carl XIV. During his reign Denn was defeated and Norway anne to Sweden, the former only reg ing independence in 1905. Up the beginning of the XX cen Sweden was one of the poo countries in Europe and had, a with Ireland and Norway, the h est number of emigrants, From middle of the XIX century onw however, the foundations of S den's highly democratic wel state were laid. During the World Wars the country remai neutral and in sixty years of Sc Democrat rule, numerous socia forms have been instituted have made Sweden one of the n efficient welfare states in the wo Sweden became a member of European Community, together Finland and Austria, in January 1

Fort of Bohus, near Göteborg, goes back to the 13th century and has recently become the spectacular setting for an *n-air theatre.*

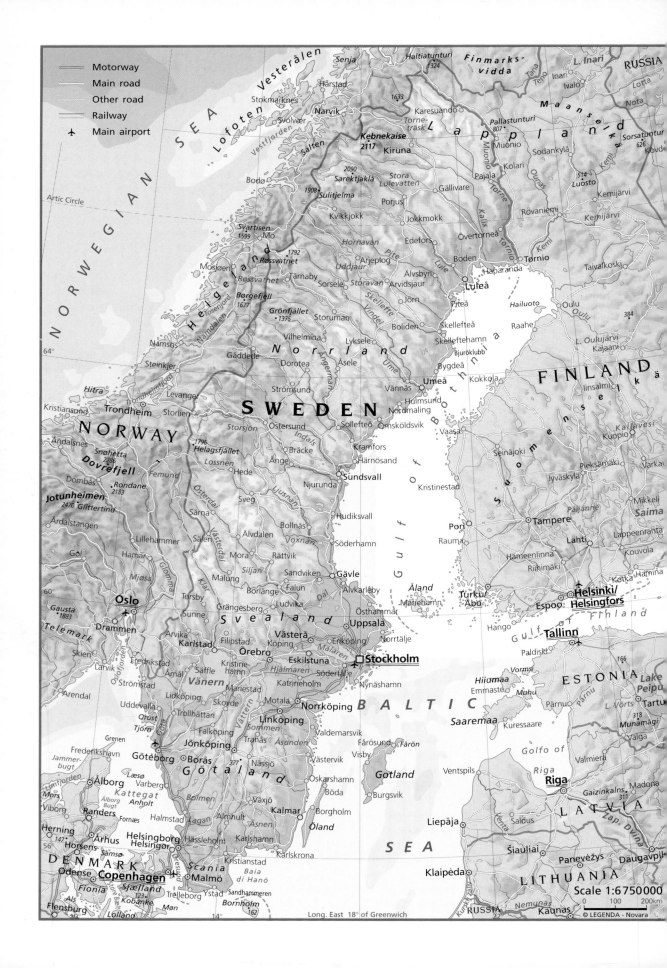